See Right Here

Inspirational Poems by a Man of God

Calvin Boone

SEE RIGHT HERE POEMS

Copyright © 2018 by Calvin Boone

All rights reserved. No part of this book may be reproduced or transmitted in any form or by any means without written permission from the author.

ISBN: 978-1-7327674-2-3
Library of Congress Control Number: 2018959320

Printed in the USA by The Vision to Fruition Publishing House
(www.vision-fruition.com)

In Memory Of

MY MOTHER GENEVA BOONE

MY SISTER JANET MARIE BOONE

In Loving Memory

Those we love don't go away
They walk beside us everyday
Unseen, unheard, but always near
Still loved, still missed and very dear

Table of Contents

Foreword

Introduction

I Came from Dirt

Jesus Called

Lord I Believe I Struck It Rich

Jesus Is My Top Shelf

A Wondering Man

Think U Not Blessed U Woke Up This Morning

Lord Pull Me Straight

People Will Talk

Holding Hands

Sleeping Is

When I Played Tennis with Jesus

God's TV

Mrs. Felicia

Mr. and Mrs. Unity

Things I Prefer

My Wife I Need Her

When We Pray to God for That Mate

Heard What U Said, Saw What U Done

Thank you God for Giving Me a Hug

Open Your Eyes to See

Walking Away Meant You Weren't Going to Stay

Stop Waiting, Now Is the Time

If It Wasn't for God, Where Would I Be?

Dedication

First of all, I dedicate this book to the Father, Son and the Holy Spirit. For without the anointing, See Right Here Poems would not have been written.

I dedicate this book also to my lovely wife, Anita Boone of whom I have been married to for twenty-seven years and more to come. She has been a rock of support to me and my family. Thanks honey, I love you and I thank God for allowing me to find you.

Whoso findeth a wife, findeth a good thing, and obtaineth favour of the Lord.
Proverbs 18:22 (KJV)

I dedicate the poem Mrs. Felicia to Mrs. Felicia, one of my former Assistant Directors of Drama (VCMI). She was very inspirational and motivated me to become better in my gift.

I dedicate the poem Mr. and Mrs. Unity to my Pastors, Apostles Tony and Cynthia Brazelton, my spiritual Mom and Dad. They have been a tremendous blessing to my wife and I and our marriage. May God Bless you!

Last of all, I dedicate this book to my mother, Geneva Boone (deceased), Lee Ernest Boone (deceased) and my sister, Janet Marie Boone (deceased), my two daughters, Tonia and Stacy, four grandkids, Princess, PJ, Alex and JR and to my brothers and family. To my church family and all my friends and anyone who choose to read See Right Here Poems, my hope is that they will gain inspiration in making a difference in this world.

To God Be the Glory!

Foreword

It is truly an honor to write this foreword for an amazing and powerful man of God. I have had the pleasure of working alongside Calvin in the Drama Ministry within our church for several years. During this time Calvin has stayed faithful, dedicated, and committed. His love for God is evident by the way he demonstrates love towards people. Over the years Calvin has written many short poems that reflect God's heart toward His people and Calvin's love for God. In addition, he has managed to capture short poems on those whom he has labored with in the faith and the ministry. These refreshing poems are uplifting and inspiring and expose the pureness of Calvin's heart. I am extremely proud of Calvin for being obedient to the instructions of God in compiling his poems into a book of poetry. Through Calvin's obedience and act of faith I believe that each person who reads this book will be motivated to pursue after the thing that God has impressed upon you to fulfill!

To God Be the Glory!
Tameka Sanders

Introduction

See Right Here Poems is a book of inspirational poems with a powerful message for the reader if he or she chooses to capture the message of hope symbolized in the Dove is flying over and that is to See Right Here Poems.

According to the biblical story in Genesis 8:11, a dove was released by Noah after the flood in order to find land; it came back carrying a freshly plucked olive leaf, a sign of life after the flood and of God bringing Noah, his family and the animals to land. So, you see the Dove carries a powerful message, if you are willing to see what is in his mouth. I feel this book carries a message pertaining to some of life's issues but when we know where we came from, it causes us to see life in a different light.

The title of the book came by me calling someone about my poems and they wanted to know what the book title would be. I told them I didn't have a title yet and they told me I would need one. So, I said to them, let me see here and the book title came slowly out as See Right Here Poems.

Take a look inside.

Psalm 91 (KJV)

¹ He that dwelleth in the secret place of the most High shall abide under the shadow of the Almighty.

² I will say of the Lord, He is my refuge and my fortress: my God; in Him will I trust.

³ Surely, He shall deliver thee from the snare of the fowler, and from the noisome pestilence.

⁴ He shall cover thee with his feathers, and under his wings shalt thou trust: his truth shall be thy shield and buckler.

⁵ Thou shalt not be afraid for the terror by night; nor for the arrow that flieth by day;

⁶ Nor for the pestilence that walketh in darkness; nor for the destruction that wasteth at noonday.

⁷ A thousand shall fall at thy side, and ten thousand at thy right hand; but it shall not come nigh thee.

⁸ Only with thine eyes shalt thou behold and see the reward of the wicked.

⁹ Because thou hast made the Lord, which is my refuge, even the most High, thy habitation;

¹⁰ There shall no evil befall thee, neither shall any plague come nigh thy dwelling.

¹¹ For he shall give his angels charge over thee, to keep thee in all thy ways.

¹² They shall bear thee up in their hands, lest thou dash thy foot against a stone.

¹³ Thou shalt tread upon the lion and adder: the young lion and the dragon shalt thou trample under feet.

¹⁴ Because he hath set his love upon me, therefore will I deliver him: I will set him on high, because he hath known my name.

¹⁵ He shall call upon me, and I will answer him: I will be with him in trouble; I will deliver him and honor him.

¹⁶ With long life will I satisfy him and shew him my salvation.

I Came from Dirt

Poem

I came from dirt, but it was by His works
He created me and I'm here for the whole world to see;
He molded all of us and this is why we need to put all our trust;
In the One who allowed me to see,
In the One who allowed me to be,
In the One who made me free,

So, go ahead and pick up some dirt,
Look at it and know that it took some powerful work,
To create you, to create me and we are unique,
I came from dirt, but my relatives are the
Father, the Son and the Holy Spirit.
I came from Dirt!

Nugget

We all came from dirt and we pray by His grace. We have become so much more, in Jesus name. Amen!

Your Thoughts

Jesus Called

Poem

Where were you when the light came on?
Were you still somewhere in the dark trying to answer your phone;
If you weren't with David who made the Giant fall then I am afraid;
You have no excuse for not answering this call;

Jesus loves us so much that He gave us ears to hear
But if we don't wake up, we won't even come near;
Near to hearing what the Master has to say;
Important stuff we need day to day;

Remember, Jesus shared His food with our pastors – Mom and Dad;
So that they could grow, and they passed it on so we as Christians would know;
When He calls me I will answer, I'll be somewhere listening for His call.

Nugget

Note that, we are swift to answer the phone when the tax man calls, when our friends and family call, I pray that we all are as swift to answer when Jesus calls.

Your Thoughts

Story

The poem Jesus Called got its start by Pastor Cynthia asking the congregation, what were we doing with the Word of God that we were receiving from VCMI? She also asked were we speaking back to some of the issues and situations we came upon?

A few days after Pastor Cynthia asked these questions, a situation arose on the metro train on my way to work, I was sitting next to three young ladies and they had the spirit of cursing in them. Every other word was a curse word. I felt in my spirit that Jesus was calling upon me to stand up to this situation.

I paused for a moment thinking if I spoke to them about their cursing, they would curse me out. At about the same time, one of the young ladies brushed up against me and with a soft pleasing voice said, "I'm so sorry, please forgive me sir." I knew this was the sign Jesus wanted me to speak to them so I said to them, "Why are you all cussing in this manner? And look at the young men laughing at you." I told them that they were three attractive young ladies and it didn't look good for them to be speaking that way. I also told them when the young men get ready for marriage, they would not marry them but someone else. I spoke Proverbs 18:21 (KJV) to them – *"Death and life are in the power of the tongue and they that love it shall eat the fruit thereof."*

I prayed for them and they asked me if I had a Bible to show them Proverbs 18:21. I showed them the scripture and asked them to see if they could go one day without cursing and they said, "they would." I also told them that it could be done because Jesus had delivered me from the spirit of cursing. They got off the train with a different spirit and I have the faith to believe they overcame this cursing spirit. The blessing came not too long after I answered Jesus Call, my wife and me were anointed as deacons.

To God Be the Glory!!!

Lord I Believe I Struck It Rich!

Poem

Lord when I was a young man
I used to find things throughout my day;
And when I would find them, I would say;
Lord, I believe I struck it Rich!

But now that I am an older man;
And have the wisdom that You gave;
I know that I was always Rich;
And in You, I am Rich today;

Lord, You gave me family
Lord, You taught me how to pray;
And even today when I find a shapely rock or stick;
It's in You that I struck it Rich,

Money ain't everything
It helps me to buy the things I need;
But when I don't have money and feel a little sick;
It's good to know in You, I struck it Rich.

To God be the Glory!

Nugget

Note that, we may have a nice house, nice car, good education and money in the bank but just remember it is in Him and through Him (Jesus) we've all, struck it rich.

Your Thoughts

Jesus is My Top Shelf

Poem

There was a once upon a time when I was doing quite well but not exactly myself
I thought I had a little friend that I would pull from the top shelf;
Until I woke up and found myself out on the street;
Walking around for days, not having anything to eat;

Living out of trash cans, food I would say;
People making comments like, Is he okay?
Jesus please forgive me for I got a little weak;
And Lord if you are watching me, I'm not that neat;

It all came about because of my weakness for the drink;
Having so much of it, I couldn't think;
Then one day, this man came to me and he said,
"If you continue to drink of this, you will be dead;
I realize this man was Jesus and I thought heavily about what He said;

So, all of those times when I walked into that store;
He was with me as I came through the door;
And all of those times when I felt alone and by myself;
I should not have reached for that bottle;
But for Jesus who is my Top Shelf.

Nugget

Note that when things are at their worst and you feel it's not getting better, you should not rely on the bottle, drugs or people giving you wrong information. Make Jesus your top shelf for advice.

Your Thoughts

A Wondering Man

Poem

Why do people sit down when they can stand up?
Why do people take lives, instead of saving lives?
Why do people steal instead of going out and doing a good will?
Why won't people be the people that God has chosen to see the people?

That need the people to step it up and free the people;
So, these are some things that a Wondering Man wonders about;
If I'm wondering about such things
What do you think God is wondering about?

Nugget

Note that, it is hard not to wonder about all the things that are going on in this world today but why not wonder about what God needs us to do to change such things.

Your Thoughts

Think U Not Blessed U Woke Up This Morning

Poem

It could have been u
Lying on that cold bed
It could have been u they considered dead
But I said, "No."

That is not the way it will go
For I have already taken the ultimate test
Died on the Cross for my children
Whom I consider my best.

So u think u not Blessed
I woke u up this morning
And this is not said to be a warning
For u know that I am so true.

Which only means, I have something left
For u to do
Not to leave u in a tizzy
Get busy (Selah).

To God be the Glory!

Nugget

Note that when u think u not blessed, think of all the good things (Jesus) has done for you and me. They are enormous!!! Plus, He woke us up this morning.

Your Thoughts

Lord Pull Me Straight

Poem

Lord, I'm tired of going down that crooked road
Tired of carrying that heavy load
I said, "No to the devil, I got good food on my plate"
So, Lord, please pull me straight.

Lord, I had taken all I could take
Because of You, I can see a new day
When all I needed to do was pray
And believe that You would pull me straight.

For Lord, it was always in Your plans for me to be a Godly man
So today, I'm driving for God and know that I'm in His plans
Because some roads are crooked, and some roads are straight
Please choose God that's all it takes.

Nugget

Always remember, God has your back. As long as you have the Word of God and Jesus in your life and have the faith to believe, all of your crooked roads are straight!!!

Your Thoughts

People Will Talk

Poem
People will talk
People will say
People will do but that's okay

I love you now
I love you still and as a matter of fact
I'll always will

Never said, I was perfect
Never will be, but everyone has faults same as me
The only one I know who is as perfect as can be

Is our Lord Jesus Christ
Who died to make us free

Nugget
You may as well come to the conclusion that people are going to talk about you. Some of it will be good and some of it will be bad but don't let it derail you from moving forward. Remember the most important thing is what God is saying about you.

Your Thoughts

Holding Hands

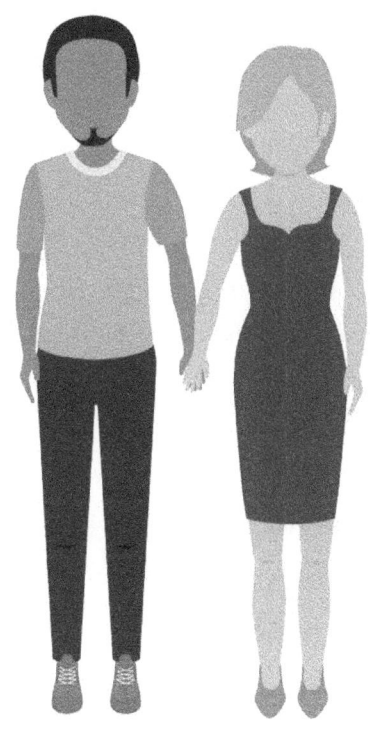

Poem

Just the other day, I was on my way to work
This comes just after that night being in church
I told the Lord I was available to do whatever He wanted me to do
Then came along this couple holding hands, smiling at each other happy as can be.

The Lord touched me to tell them, He was so happy to see people holding hands, sharing His love the way it was meant to be
I also told them that this showing of affection would help me and my wife keep moving in the right direction

Nugget

Holding hands, I feel is very important to God. It is very important in our love walk because God is all about love and making that connection. It causes us when we pray to touch and in Jesus name, I pray, agree. It can be a world changer. Each one reach one. Matthew 18:20 (KJV) – "For where two or three are gathered together in my name, there am I in the midst of them."

Your Thoughts

Sleeping Is

Poem

Sleeping is quiet
Sleeping is good
Sleeping is something, you should
Get plenty of rest

Keep sleep close to your chest
So, you will be able to do your best
Saying goodnight and your sleep goes right
Means the next day, you won't be uptight

Sleeping is quite
Sleeping is great
Sleeping is something
I just can't wait

Nugget

Sleeping, peace and rest are all relatives of God. When we are sleeping and at peace, we will receive rest. Then we are energized to do the work God has for us.

Your Thoughts

When I Played Tennis with Jesus

Poem

When I played tennis with Jesus
He beat me with love
And I felt so much better afterwards
For you see, it was all about love

In the beginning of the match, there was love
In the middle of the match, there was love
And at the end of the match, there was love

No hate but love
15 Love
30 Love
40 Love
Game, Set, Match
Love
How can you not feel better after being beat by Jesus
With Love
To God Be the Glory!

Nugget

When I played tennis with Jesus, He beat me with love. Since Jesus is our creator and He is all about love then love is what we will see and receive from Him so, whenever we are playing any sport like basketball, football, baseball, golf, soccer, hockey, volleyball and boxing, remember, at the end of the game or match, whether you win or lose, show your opponent love.

Your Thoughts

God's TV

Poem

I see so many of my people striving to get fame
Don't they know that fame only comes through Jesus name?
So many people trying to become stars
Don't they know that they have always been my stars?

So many people trying to get on the red carpet
Don't they know that the blood of Jesus is their red carpet?
So many people are trying hard to get on TV
Don't they know that they have always been on God's TV
every single day of their lives?

Even before they were born, I have been watching them and will never turn the channel
God's TV is for all His children and all of His stars are in Heaven.

Nugget

Remember, God sees everything we do. He hears everything we say so He has been watching us on His TV even before we were formed in our mother's womb. So, we are already famous because we are His children and seen on His TV.

Your Thoughts

Mrs. Felicia

Poem

Mrs. Felicia, you are quite the teacher
Ministering drama to us as God's chosen preacher
You are very talented in what you do
Working long hours, seeing the Lord's mission thru

Because you check on us to make sure, we're in place
Shows us how much you really care about us winning this race
Thank you for taking your precious time
Working with us to get down our lines

Stressing voice projection and moving us in all kinds of directions
Not only for us but for the congregation's protection
Because if they can't receive it then how are they to believe it to be true
The message that God wants to come thru us by using His powerful people
Same as you.

Nugget

If you are in the Drama Ministry at your church or any other ministries of God, you need someone to direct you, lead you to where God needs you to be and to do. You need someone to invest their time and love to the point where it touches your heart where you are able to put into action the message your pastor is preaching by using your godly gifts.

Your Thoughts

Mr. and Mrs. Unity

Poem

When I look at them this is what I see
Mr. and Mrs. Unity.
Thank you, Lord through you they have come to be

Mr. and Mrs. Unity
Lord, they work hard for you
They work hard for me
They work hard for all your people to become free

They are good examples of how You want your married couples to be
Walking in love for thee
I see them Lord and I know the message they carry from You is not fake.

But we as your people need to participate in order to get the good
Word that tastes like ice cream and cake
I thank you Lord for giving not only me but all your people
And the whole world to see. The message they carry from the heart
(love) from You that stings like a bee
The good examples like Mr. and Mrs. Unity.

Nugget

The definition of Unity – the state of being united or joined as a whole, oneness. When you are having problems in your marriage and your family don't see eye to eye. Maybe your friends don't want to be your friend anymore. Remember, God is all about love.

Jeremiah 3:15 (KJV)

And I will give you pastors according to mine heart, which shall feed you with knowledge and understanding.

I'm so glad He sent me, Mr. and Mrs. Unity, Pastors/Apostles Tony and Cynthia Brazelton.

Your Thoughts

Story

The poem Mr. and Mrs. Unity got its start by my wife and I attending Bible Study on Wednesday night. Towards the end of Bible Study, it was mentioned to the congregation that there would be stations set up in the lobby with a camera and mic because they wanted each person to think of one word that best described our pastors. It was then that the Lord dropped the word 'Unity' into my spirit. I mentioned this to my wife, what the Lord had done and we both agreed that 'Unity' was the word that best described them. It was not too long after this event that Jesus had me write the poem, Mr. and Mrs. Unity to give a snapshot of what our pastors are all about and that is, doing the business of the Kingdom.

To God Be the Glory!

Things I Prefer

Poem

I prefer to have God in my life.
I prefer to be someone who is nice.
I prefer to follow God's son Jesus Christ.
I prefer to make many a sacrifice.

I prefer to do the right thing.
I prefer to worship the King.
I prefer to bless Him when I sing.
I prefer to have peaceful dreams.

I prefer to thank Him for each day
I prefer to include this when I pray
I prefer,

Lord Have Your Way!!!

Nugget

Remember, you can prefer to do this, or you can prefer to do that. God gives us a choice and I pray that we prefer the things of God.

Your Thoughts

My Wife I Need Her

Poem

My wife I need her to love me
My wife I need her to be free
My wife I need her to be able to see

I need her to stay on track
I need her to cover my back
I need her when it's time to react

Guess what?

I got and received what I needed in my wife
A wife who is gentle and so nice
A wife who won't quit and continues to fight

Thank you, God, for opening my eyes to see
The wife You had and wanted for me
for You knew there would be nothing sweeter than
My lovely wife, Anita

Nugget

I Need My Wife to Complete Me. Genesis 2:23 – *Adam said, This is now bone of my bones, and flesh of my flesh: she shall be called Woman, because she was taken out of Man.* I am loving the gift God gave to me because He created her for me and don't you think God knows what He is doing?
He is God!!!

Your Thoughts

When We Pray to God for That Mate

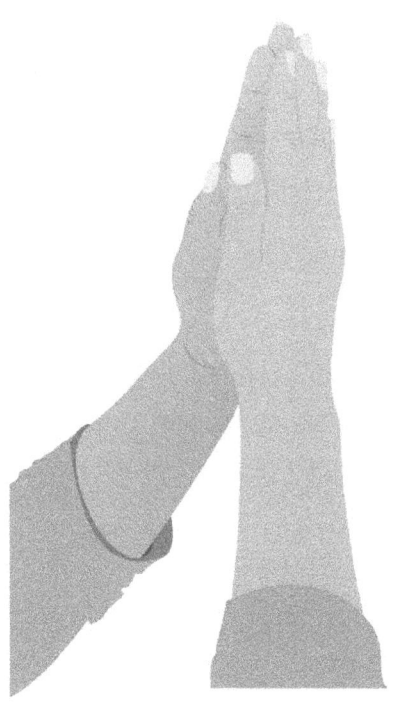

Poem

When We Pray to God for that Mate
He knows exactly who we need so we won't have to go
on 10 to 12 dates
He knows when they will come and how long it will take
He puts all the ingredients in them as if He has baked us a cake

Now if only He can get us to partake,
and not want to bake our own cake
Because we are impatient and not wanting to wait
We choose the icing and the wrong cake

Why won't we let Him handle this because He knows
What it takes
But we mess it up and will continue to wait

Nugget

Remember when you pray and ask God for your mate trust Him to give you His best because He wants the best for us. If you check out their heart, it will be the heart of God. The heart will get you into places where looks won't.

Your Thoughts

Heard What U Said, Saw What U Done

Poem

I heard what u said, saw what u done
but I still love u and God wants me
to experience joy and to have fun
He knows it wasn't u but the spirit in u

That did it but His hope is that u get yourself together
so, the God in u will admit it
I pray u move forward so u can receive peace of mind
so, God can use u in this place and in this time. Selah

To God be The Glory!

Nugget

Remember, we are not perfect and will make mistakes, but God gives us a chance to repent and ask for forgiveness. The key is to walk in love.

Acts 3:19 (KJV) – *Repent ye therefore, and be converted, that your sins may be blotted out, when the times of refreshing shall come from the presence of the Lord.*

Your Thoughts

Thank You God for Giving Me a Hug

Poem

Thank You God for Giving Me a Hug

I thank You God for giving me a hug for I know when You hugged me it came straight from above

It made me feel the power of love and how You want me to go out and hug

I realize sometimes we may not feel or receive the love from (some) family or friends

but You are always there and will be there to the end.

I thank you God for Your precious love and (most of all)

I thank you God for giving me a hug.

To God Be the Glory!

Nugget

Remember to show your Godly love through your hugs. By hugging family, friends, neighbors, the homeless, just hug people. It can have an effect throughout this world. It can change someone's day, life and perception on whether people really care or not.

Your Thoughts

Open Your Eyes to See

Poem

Open your eyes to see
What is yours and have
always been meant to be
You may not be able to see it
because you are in a forest amongst the trees
But God has a power saw (The Word)
that will cut them down to your knees
so that you are able to see the prize that is yours and also for me
The prize that has always been meant to be, if you are ready to
receive the Father, the Son and the Holy Spirit!!!

To God Be the Glory!!!

Nugget

It is very important that our eyes are clearly open so that we are seeing what God needs us to see so we can determine our path, get our directions on where we need to go, who we need to reach and impact the world to bring about positive change.

2 King 6:17 (KJV)

And Elisha prayed, and said, Lord, I pray thee, open his eyes, that he may see. And the Lord opened the eyes of the young man; and he saw: and, behold, the mountain was full of horses and chariots of fire round about Elisha.

Your Thoughts

Walking Away Meant You Weren't Going to Stay

Poem

When I saw you walk away, it was my reality that you weren't going to stay.
Funny how you didn't even give me a chance to say,
"Why are you walking away?"

I remember the times we had together and the things we used to say.
Like, "I will never leave you or walk away."
But I remind myself and you on this day that when you see someone walking away, that means they weren't going to stay.

To God Be the Glory!!!

Nugget

Remember – People walk out of your life for a reason but when you accept Jesus as your personal Lord and Savior, He is there for all seasons.

Matthews 28:20 (KJV)
I will never leave or forsake you. I will be with you always even unto the end of time.

Your Thoughts

Stop Waiting, Now Is the Time

Poem
Stop Waiting, Now is the Time
God has something for you, but you say
This is not mine

Could it be that someone gave you that,
"Who do you think you are?" look that is holding
You back?
Well, God wants you to give them that
"I am a child of God!" look and get back on track

Note that we all have red lights in our lives that will
cause us to stop and wait but God will use this to make sure we
get to our destination safe

The coast is clear, stop waiting now is the time
Go get and deliver what God has for you and say
to yourself, it's mine.

To God Be the Glory!!!

Nugget
Remember – God is Sovereign, and His timing is perfect!

Ecclesiastes 3:1 (KJV)
To everything there is a season, and a time to every purpose under the heaven.

Your Thoughts

If It Wasn't for God, Where Would I Be?

Poem

If it wasn't for God, Where Would I Be?
I wouldn't be here, I wouldn't be me
I wouldn't be able to talk
I wouldn't be able to walk
I wouldn't be able to see what God has coming for me
I wouldn't be able to hear that awesome sound
when He comes back to earth and touches the ground

Where would I be?
So, if it wasn't for God, I would not
have been able to see
that His Son, Jesus Christ died on the Cross to set me free.

To God Be the Glory!!!

Nugget

Remember – It is because of God that we have our being

Psalm 124:2 (KJV)

If it had not been the Lord who was on our side, when men rose up against us

Your Thoughts

Acknowledgements

I want to take this time to thank my God for blessing, healing and keeping me. I give Him all the Praise, all the Glory, all the Honor and inspiration for being able to write "See Right Here Poems," To God Be the Glory. I like to thank my Pastors/Apostles Tony and Cynthia Brazelton for being such good role models of God. I thank them for praying for my wife, Anita and me. James 5:16 (KJV) - *The effectual fervent prayer of a righteous man availeth much.* I dedicate the poem/Mr. and Mrs. Unity to them, "Much Love."

To my lovely wife, Anita, I thank you for being my wife for 27 years and more to come. You have been an inspiration and a rock of support and this is why I'm dedicating my book to my God and you.

I like to thank Mrs. Darlene for being such an inspiration to me and everyone in the Drama Ministry and you all know who you are with the love of God for inspiring me to show the Word of God in action. Much love to Mrs. Tricie who brings everything and everyone together with the power of God's love, so we are ready to produce the gifts from God. I dedicate the poem, Mrs. Felicia to Mrs. Felicia. Thank you for your inspiration and dedication.

To my Mom and Dad, family and friends, I thank you all for your love and support. To my good friends Sharon and Dave, I would also like to thank you all so much for your love and support. To Sharon's mom Joan who has transitioned to be with the Lord, I thank

God that he spoke through her always asking me the question, "When are you going to write that book?"

To the Deacon Ministry, Fishers of Men (FOM) and Mighty Men of Valor (MMOV) Ministry, much love to all of you. I would also like to thank Tameka Sanders for graciously writing the Foreword. I would like to especially thank Minister Keshia Freeland, for when I was looking for someone to publish my book, she suggested that I contact Minister LaKesha L. Williams. I thank Minister LaKesha of Vision to Fruition Publishing for her help in bringing this book to completion in Jesus Name, Amen.

To God Be the Glory!

About the Author

Calvin Boone is a Deacon at Victory Christian Ministries International (VCMI).

He was born to the parents, Geneva and Lee Ernest Boone in Newport News, VA in 1953 and was raised in Conway, NC. To know Calvin is to experience his keen sense of humor, a spirit of laughter and love of people. He has a passion for working with the homeless, elderly and serving his community. He also enjoys singing praises to God.

He is a faithful husband, father of two children, Tonia and Stacy and four grandchildren Princess, PJ, Alex and JR. He has been married for twenty-seven years to his wife, Anita Boone. Currently, Calvin resides in Southern Maryland and he served in the Drama Ministry as a Minister of Drama and received the Catch Award in 2011 for his faithfulness. He is a member of the Mighty Men of Valor (MMOV) and Fishers of Men (FOM). Calvin is a Veteran of the United States Army. His work history includes the former Greater Southeast Community Hospital. He also worked at Electronic Data Systems (EDS) for eleven years.

His last place of employment was with the Federal Trade Commission (FTC) and after 16 years of service at the (FTC), he retired and received a Meritorious Award in 2016. He also served three years in the United States Army and has a total of 19 years of United States Government service.

He enjoys playing and watching tennis, basketball, and baseball. His favorite baseball teams are the New York Yankees and the Washington Nationals. His favorite tennis players are Serena Williams and Roger Federer. He also likes watching his favorite team the Washington Redskins, but his Heavenly Father is Jesus Christ and without Him, none of the above would be possible.

About the Publisher

At The Vision to Fruition Publishing House, we are dedicated to helping others bring their publishing visions to fruition.

Whether it's as grand as a book you want to write, a business you want to start, a conference or event you want to host, a ministry you want to launch or an organization you want to start; or as small as needing a computer repair, logo design or web design; The Vision to Fruition Group will help you walk through the process and set you up for success! At The Vision to Fruition Group we don't have clients, we have Visionaries. We provide solutions to equip others to pursue their visions & dreams with reckless abandon.

Since 2018 we have published more than twenty-three authors, eight of which were Amazon Bestsellers. We would love for you to join our family of Visionaries as well!!!

Learn more here: www.vision-fruition.com

www.ingramcontent.com/pod-product-compliance
Lightning Source LLC
Chambersburg PA
CBHW020917090426
42736CB00008B/674